Emotional Intelligence Mastery

Why EQ is Important for Success and Matters More Than IQ

By: Travis Wells and Daniel Gillihan

© Copyright 2019 by Pardi Publishing - All rights reserved.

This document is geared towards providing exact and reliable information in regards to the topic and issue covered. The publication is sold with the idea that the publisher is not required to render accounting, officially permitted, or otherwise, qualified services. If advice is necessary, legal or professional, a practiced individual in the profession should be ordered.

From a Declaration of Principles which was accepted and approved equally by a Committee of the American Bar Association and a Committee of Publishers and Associations.

In no way is it legal to reproduce, duplicate, or transmit any part of this document in either electronic means or in printed format. Recording of this publication is strictly prohibited and any storage of this document is not allowed unless with written permission from the publisher. All rights reserved.

The information provided herein is stated to be truthful and consistent, in that any liability, in terms of inattention or otherwise, by any usage or abuse of any policies, processes, or directions contained within is the solitary and utter responsibility of the recipient reader. Under no circumstances will any legal responsibility or blame be held against the publisher for any reparation, damages, or monetary loss due to the information herein, either directly or indirectly.

Respective authors own all copyrights not held by the publisher.

The information herein is offered for informational purposes solely, and is universal as so. The presentation of the information is without contract or any type of guarantee assurance.

The trademarks that are used are without any consent, and the publication of the trademark is without permission or backing by the trademark owner. All trademarks and brands within this book are for clarifying purposes only and are the owned by the owners themselves, not affiliated with this document.

Table of Contents

INTRODUCTION 1
DISCUSSION 2
PART 1: WHAT IS EMOTIONAL INTELLIGENCE 3
    Chapter 1 – Emotions: What are Emotions? 4
    Chapter 2 – What is Emotional Intelligence? 6
    Chapter 3 – EQ Versus IQ 8
    Chapter 4 – Benefits of Emotional Intelligence 11
    Chapter 5 – What Characteristics Define an Emotionally Intelligent Person? 15
    Chapter 6 – Real Life Case Studies 16
PART 2: EMOTIONAL INTELLIGENCE IN ACTION 19
    Chapter 7 – An Action Plan to Increase Your Emotional Intelligence 20
PART 3: DISCOVER THE POWER OF YOUR OWN INNER STRENGTH 24
    Chapter 8 – Mastering Self-Awareness 25
    Chapter 9 – How to Identify Your Strengths and Weaknesses 28
    Chapter 10 – How to Improve Motivation, Avoid Procrastination and Distractions 30
    Chapter 11 – The Importance of Confidence and How to Increase It 39
PART 4: SELF-MANAGEMENT: HOW TO CONTROL YOUR EMOTIONS 44
    Chapter 12 – How to Manage and Conquer Out-of-Control Emotions 45

Chapter 13 – Expressing Healthy Emotions 47

Chapter 14 – How to Control Anger and Use It in a Positive Way 49

Chapter 15 – How to React to Tough Situations with Resilience 50

Chapter 16 – How to Free Yourself from Other People's Opinions and Judgment 52

Chapter 17 – How to Deal with Criticism 56

PART 5: HOW TO CONNECT WITH OTHERS AND IMPROVE RELATIONSHIPS 60

Chapter 18 – How to Understand and Connect with Others on a Deeper Level 61

Chapter 19 – Winning with People 1: How to Analyze People 63

Chapter 20 – Winning with People 2: Why Social Skills Matter 65

Chapter 21 – Winning with People 3: How to Communicate Effectively 67

Chapter 22 – What is Manipulation, How it Works 71

Chapter 23 – Mastering Positive Manipulation 74

PART 6: EMOTIONAL INTELLIGENCE IN PRACTICE 85

Chapter 24 – Practical Exercises 86

Chapter 25 – How to Use Emotional Intelligence Skills in Real World Situations 88

CONCLUSION 90

Introduction

There have been many discoveries in the past couple of decades touching on what it takes to be successful in this ever-changing dynamic world. Most of us would be familiar with IQ or intelligence quotient, which is the most common and widely known measure of human intelligence. It's commonly accepted that IQ is the key determining factor for achieving success in the workplace. But recently, it was discovered that 70% of the time, people with average IQs performed better than those with higher IQs in the workplace.

It is generally accepted that emotional intelligence is a crucial factor for achieving success in the workplace and life today. Emotional intelligence is the ability to identify emotions in yourself and other people around you and manage them in a beneficial and rewarding way. Emotional intelligence refers to a set of critical skills needed to succeed in business, professional, social, and personal life. These skills are necessary to navigate the ever-changing socio-economic landscape successfully. This book aims to provide you with comprehensive and concise information of everything you need to know about emotional intelligence, why it's necessary, and what steps you need to take to improve your emotional intelligence to excel in whatever endeavor you take on in life.

Discussion

This book aims to provide readers with comprehensive but concise information about everything there is to know about emotional intelligence. It contains information about all the skills associated with emotional intelligence such as self-awareness, self-confidence, how to connect with people better, persuasion skills, and many more.

Each person has some degree of emotional intelligence in them already. It's a good idea to be aware of where you stand as you read this book. Some people may already have a high level of EQ and a good understanding of the basics of emotional intelligence. In that case, you may wish to learn more about emotional intelligence to strengthen your EQ further. There may be others who do not know the basics yet and may need guidance on how to get started. Whichever category you fall in, we trust and hope that you will be able to find something of value in this book that can help you become a more emotionally intelligent and successful person.

Part 1: What is Emotional Intelligence

Chapter 1 – Emotions: What are Emotions?

Emotion is a psychological state which is often associated with feelings, thoughts, or moods. We experience many different emotions every day, which are triggered by events happening around us. The emotions we experience are what shapes our behavior. Behavior refers to the way we act around others. Emotions can influence our behavior in many ways. Personality, on the other hand, refers to the unique combination of emotional and behavioral patterns. In this section, we will explore how we can gain awareness of our emotions, label them, and gain a better understanding of ourselves through self-study.

The task of identifying and labeling emotions is not as easy as it sounds. Emotions consist of not only several common emotions that we often hear about such as happiness, sadness, or anger; there are also more complex emotions like calmness, contentment, humiliation, isolation, passion, adoration, and many more. Learning and understanding these emotions can be a good starting point if you are not already familiar with most of them.

You can also categorize most emotions into six categories: joy, surprise, sadness, anger, disgust, and fear. Getting to know about all these emotions in depth will make it easier for you to identify them when they manifest in your life. This exercise serves two purposes: recognizing emotions in yourself and other people. This helps put you in a better position to manage and utilize them to achieve your goals.

The emotions we experience are often triggered by external events or situations. They may appear together with other emotions or as a combination of emotions. For instance, the feeling of being hopeful is a combination of anticipation and trust, while the emotion of delight is a combination of joy and surprise.

Take note of how these emotions are triggered and what the effects are. They may trigger other emotions, creating some sort of chain reaction. Emotions can be very complex and may be built upon multiple layers of related emotions. How will they affect the subsequent actions people take? When you get into an argument with someone, how do you feel? When someone raises their voice at you, what emotions do you experience? Is it hurt, stress, anger, or a combination of these? How does it affect your work? Try and think about all this the next time an emotion is triggered within you. You can even try it out now. Do you recognize any emotions you are experiencing at the moment? We will continue the discussion about emotions in Chapter 8, where we will dig deeper into self-awareness.

Chapter 2 – What is Emotional Intelligence?

Emotional intelligence is a relatively new concept which was first introduced in a 1964 research paper by psychology professor Michael Beldoch. The idea was expanded in another paper in 1990 by psychologists Peter Salovey and John Mayer. The term emotional intelligence was described as having four key branches:

1. Nonverbal recognition of emotions (perceiving emotions)
2. Utilization of emotions in cognitive thinking
3. Understanding emotions (and their resulting actions)
4. Managing emotions

Both Salovey and Mayer believed that emotional intelligence is a form of human intelligence alongside cognitive intelligence, creativity, and others. The four branches or levels of emotional intelligence are commonly classified as the ability model. This means that people are measured based on their abilities on each of the four branches. The four branches are arranged in such a way where the first branch concerns the most basic form of mental process and moves on down to more complex psychological integrated processes. These levels would later be modified as a result of further research by the authors.

The term emotional intelligence became well known only in 1995 when science journalist, Daniel Goleman, released the best-seller book called Emotional Intelligence. Goleman claimed that emotional intelligence is more crucial to business success than cognitive intelligence. He listed five key concepts in emotional intelligence:

1. **Self-Awareness.** The awareness of one's own emotions, weaknesses, strengths, and motivations, and their impact on other people.
2. **Self-Regulation.** The ability to manage one's own emotions.
3. **Social skill.** The ability to manage relationships and lead people towards desired directions.

4. **Empathy**. The ability to intercept and understand other people's emotions.
5. **Motivation**. Having intrinsic motivation as opposed to having extrinsic motivation.

Goleman's idea of emotional intelligence would later be classified as a mixed model, which involves aspects of both ability and trait models.

Chapter 3 – EQ Versus IQ

Intelligence quotient (IQ) has been the most traditional tool for many years to assess and measure a person's purported intelligence. A person's IQ is said to indicate their level of cognitive ability and can be measured using standardized tests. These tests will assess a person's ability in various cognitive aspects such as verbal, numerical, or spatial reasoning. It aims to measure a person's problem-solving abilities, analytical and logical thinking, and memory. Before the emergence of emotional intelligence, the sum of human intelligence was thought by some to be embodied in their IQ score.

Proper IQ tests are rarely used or required by organizations today. They will normally rely on specific academic qualifications or certifications as a way to measure a person's industry-specific IQ. For example, in order for a company to hire a new computer software engineer, the candidate needs to have sufficient IQ relating to this field, therefore, they would be required to possess degrees in the field of computer science or software engineering before they can be considered for the position.

The biggest problem with IQ is that human intelligence is made up of more than just cognitive abilities. There are many other aspects of human intelligence which are not included in IQ tests, such as creativity and advanced verbal, social, and emotional skills. In the business world, a person's IQ can be said to embody their technical skills, such as quantitative aptitude or the capacity to understand complex equations or algorithms. We can see that there is no doubt that a person's IQ still plays a crucial role in a professional or academic context.

Emotional intelligence is one aspect of human intelligence that is excluded from a person's IQ. Emotional intelligence or EQ refers to the ability to recognize and manage our own emotions as well as those of others, and to incorporate this awareness into daily practice such as decision-making. Emotional intelligence involves the ability to create positive relationships with people in our professional and personal lives. It incorporates ideas such as empathy, compassion, intuition, flexibility, integrity, trust, and stress management, among other ideas.

We can use a scenario to illustrate the difference between EQ and IQ:

There is an ongoing project to build a bridge in South Africa. The region is experiencing unusually cold weather, and the workers are not prepared for it and therefore, cannot work efficiently. The project manager, who happens to be from Norway is, however, unaffected by it and wants the work to continue. He's equipped with the technical skills on how to build bridges, which includes the technical difficulties of working in extreme weather conditions. The project workers also have the technical skills required of them to perform their work well. But they may need some guidance about working in unusual weather conditions.

As of right now, the workers are unhappy and lack the motivation to work due to the cold weather. The project manager has the expertise to help his workers deal with the technical issues involved when working in extreme weather conditions. This is derived from the IQ portion of the project manager's intelligence. On the other hand, the project manager also has to deal with the workers' motivation to work under such cold conditions. First, he should be able to recognize and understand what the workers are feeling and experiencing. Secondly, he would need to know how to motivate his workers should he need the project to carry on. The abilities in this aspect are derived from the his EQ. If the project manager fails to recognize and understand the worker's uneasiness, he would carry on the project as if there's no problem. This would certainly make the workers feel upset or even angry. There is a risk that they will provide substandard work on the bridge if their needs are not addressed.

If the project manager recognizes the workers' uneasiness but fails to motivate them to continue working and provide adequate solutions, he might decide to put the project on hold until the weather improves. But now, there's also a risk that the project may not be completed on schedule. Being aware of the team's emotions and having the ability to control their behavior is a clear sign of emotional intelligence. By having a deeper understanding of the team's feelings, thoughts, and motivations, the project manager is able to better manage their behavior to the advantage of the organization and everyone else. When we understand what motivates the people in a team, their underlying emotions, and how they react to different circumstances, we can direct their behavior positively. This is the difference between IQ and EQ.

Another important distinction between EQ and IQ is that IQ is very much fixed in an individual. Our cognitive abilities are likely to remain the same after reaching adulthood. There may be ways to boost our IQ up a little, perhaps by a small percentage with the right kind of training. On the other hand, there is a lot of room for improving our EQ level. Following proper exercises can help anyone increase their EQ significantly.

Chapter 4 – Benefits of Emotional Intelligence

After we understand what it means to be emotionally intelligent, we can then look at some of the many benefits of having a sufficient level of emotional intelligence. What are the areas of life that require emotional intelligence? Which areas lack emotional intelligence more than the others? How can emotional intelligence be used to make our lives better and more meaningful? Here are some of the benefits of having a substantial amount of emotional intelligence in many different areas of life.

Leadership skills

People who are said be emotionally intelligent have a solid understanding of the people they work with. This could be an ability they have nurtured since youth, or a skill they developed later in life through years or decades of experience. This understanding goes beyond merely having a basic background knowledge of the people they work with; it goes into things which can be considered more intimate, such as understanding the emotions that motivate them.

People with a high level of emotional intelligence are able to use this information to foster loyalty among subordinates by constantly motivating them the right way. A leader such as a manager must be able to always control their workers in order to achieve the organization's both short-term and long-term goals. We know that workers need to be happy and motivated in order to work optimally.

A manager's role is not limited to only giving orders or directions to their subordinates. They also have a duty to build morale and offer encouragement whenever needed. Emotions play a role in almost every aspect of our lives, including the workplace. People at times will feel worried, dreadful, happy, bored, etc. These emotions are constantly shifting depending on situations that present themselves on a daily basis. The leader must always be ready to deal with these changes as they come and make the necessary decisions to deal with these issues.

The manager would also be required to know how to deal with a diverse range of personalities in a particular team, each with their own unique emotional make-up, emotional responses to certain situations, and motivations. By being able to understand their subordinates in such a way, the manager can create a more robust and cohesive team by knowing how to leverage the weaknesses and strengths of the team members.

Besides understanding the emotions of the people they lead, a leader should also be aware of and understand their own emotions. Emotionally intelligent leaders are able to manage their emotions and avoid letting them dictate the actions they take while at work. A manager might be facing a crisis inside or outside of work that is causing them a lot of distress. By being aware of his or her own state of mind, they can make individual decisions to avoid unnecessarily causing bigger distress to the team.

For instance, there may be a meeting that was to take place on a day the manager was under pressure. By carrying on with the meeting, they run the risk of losing their composure if things don't go well. This could have a lasting effect and could needlessly hurt the morale of the team. Alternatively, a capable manager might be aware of their own state of mind and realize that they have enough courage to maintain their composure to carry on with the meeting. When leaders have strong emotional intelligence, they can create a solid and high performing team.

Communication skills

Whether at work or at school, effective communication is a valuable skill to have. We need to be able to communicate thoughts, ideas, or instructions in the best way possible if we want the listeners to react positively.

At the most basic level, whenever we need to communicate something, we want people to understand clearly what is being communicated. It could be a suggestion, request, advice, criticism, protest, or compliment. For example, you noticed your colleague doing something which you believe could have been done in a better way. So you intend to advise or give constructive criticism to them. Without proper awareness of the surrounding circumstances and the emotions they might be experiencing, you run the risk of offending them.

Emotionally intelligent people would be able to structure the criticism in a way that would not offend the other person but would cause them to appreciate the help. Being emotionally intelligent means having the ability to communicate information in a way that will elicit the best possible response from listeners.

Resolving conflicts

One of the main reasons why emotional intelligence is such a desired attribute to have in the business world is because they often can help resolve conflicts in the most beneficial way. Conflicts often arise in almost any business sector, whether within an organization or another company. In certain industries, passions and emotions often run high. People may constantly be on edge especially if things do not turn out as planned. Disagreements about the direction of a particular product or project may arise. Miscommunication can cause deep distrust or fallout if not appropriately treated. Sometimes, we may come across clients with erratic or neurotic behavior which can potentially be disastrous if not confronted properly.

People have to be constantly ready to face conflicts in the workplace. Having high emotional intelligence can help us resolve conflict in the best way possible. With enough empathy and awareness of the emotions of people involved in a conflict, the emotionally intelligent person can be a good conflict resolution agent. By understanding the needs and motivations of the people involved, they can help settle the conflict with minimal damage and avoid a potential catastrophe. We can help avoid conflicts by having decent negotiating skills, assertiveness, and empathy.

Adaptability

Having emotional intelligence can help us adapt to changes more quickly with less difficulty. People at higher positions will have greater responsibilities placed on their shoulders. They will be required to make bigger and riskier decisions at higher levels of the company hierarchy. They will also experience more uncertainties and be expected to deal with it accordingly.

Problems and complications will always trigger negative emotions in people. Whether such complications are expected or not, the managers are required to deal with the problem and fix it. Emotionally intelligent people can deal with these issues well because whenever a setback occurs, they can manage their emotions better and will not let negative emotions get in the way of rational thinking.

Chapter 5 – What Characteristics Define an Emotionally Intelligent Person?

There are several key characteristics that define emotionally intelligent people. A person with high EQ is generally more confident, are fully aware of their true self, and understand their strengths and weaknesses. They are also able to handle challenging emotional situations.

People with high emotional intelligence are also open-minded. They are honest about what they know and what they don't know. They are more open about accepting changes and realizing new experiences.

Emotionally intelligent people are balanced. They understand the need for a good work-life balance. They know how to take care of their health and they seldom experience stress despite working hard.

People with high EQ also tend to lead by example. They understand how leading by example is a better way to influence others than merely telling them what to do.

Emotionally intelligent people know how to articulate their feelings well. They can even articulate complex emotions and describe them clearly to others.

Curiosity is another trait often found in emotionally intelligent people. They are curious about others, but not in a judgmental or negative way.

Chapter 6 – Real Life Case Studies

The best evidence to show how emotional intelligence can help ensure success in the business world is to look at the CEOs of some of the most successful companies in the world. Business individuals, especially business leaders, are often stereotyped as ruthless and profiteering. But how most of the current business leaders carry themselves would suggest that they are anything but evil. These leaders often display high levels of emotional intelligence when dealing with employees in their organization or with the public.

Jeff Bezos

The founder and CEO of the largest internet company and retailer of the world, Amazon, is known for his self-deprecating style, which helps make people feel comfortable with him. He has also shown exemplary behavior on how to deal with criticism. The New York Times published a story in 2015 which described Amazon as a mega-corporation that only strives for innovation and profits at the expense and wellbeing of its workers. The article exposed incidences of how workers are mistreated and the general treatment of its employees despite experiencing massive financial success. Bezos responded swiftly by sending out a memo to Amazon employees, encouraging them to carefully read the New York Times article and to report any similar incidences; he even invited his employees to directly reach out to him via email. He stated that even if such incidences are rare, it has to be reported because there should be no tolerance for such lack of empathy in the company. Bezos also made further changes a year later on the method it uses to assess employees' performance. In 2018, Amazon raised its minimum wage to $15 per hour for all its employees, including part-time, temporary, and seasonal employees. This amount was more than doubled the federal minimum wage, which was at $7.25 per hour at the time and will benefit more than 250,000 employees. Bezos indicated that this decision was made in response to criticism it received about unfair pay and treatment of its employees. Bezos went further than merely responding to critics; he decided to lead the way by encouraging other large employers to do the same. This is a prime example of how we should respond to criticism.

Ursula Burns

Burns was a mechanical engineering graduate who started her career as an intern at Xerox. She slowly rose through the ranks until she became the CEO of the company in 2009, becoming the first black woman to lead a Fortune 500 company. Early in her career, she learned that understanding and managing her own emotions, and reading and responding to the emotions of other people was key to achieving personal goals and changes that people wish to make in the workplace. Burns not only achieved career success, but also helped the company steer clear of bankruptcy, and lead the transformation of the company from being a photocopier manufacturer to a business outsourcing services company. She is known for being direct but respectful, as well as having a strong sense of mission and being assertive.

Elon Musk

CEO of the electric car manufacturer, Tesla, Inc. Elon Musk is another business leader who often displays signs of emotional intelligence through his words and actions. In 2017, a report was published stating that Tesla experiences 30% more factory worker injuries compared to other companies in the same industry. In response to the report, Musk indicated personal accountability and wrote a heartfelt email to Tesla workers, where he expressed sympathy and affirmed his commitment to their safety. Musk requested employees to report all injuries to him directly and decided to meet with all injured workers when they get better in order to understand how the injuries occurred and how to make working conditions safer for everyone.

Indra Nooyi

PepsiCo CEO, Indra Nooyi, wrote to the parents of 29 senior executives, telling them what their children have been doing for the company and thanking them for raising such great people, and how the company has benefitted from their services. Nooyi understood the value of its employees and that if the company wishes to hold on to its employees, it has to appeal to them through its business model and values emotionally. As soon as she became CEO of PepsiCo, she introduced the "Performance with Purpose" corporate mission, where part of the mission is to develop the workforce by creating a workplace where workers feel they can maintain a job as well as a decent life. Nooyi is a proponent of emotional intelligence, and she's aware of how projecting herself through words or actions sets the tone for the entire company. She believes in valuing and respecting employees, and she never shies from expressing it directly to them.

Alan Mullaly

The former CEO of Ford Motors was known to be one of the most emotionally intelligent business leaders. When he became CEO in 2006, he had to overcome some serious challenges facing the company. Due to major changes in the industry, Mullaly had to shift the workforce focus and transform the product line of the company. He helped create a better work environment for the employees by visiting most of the plants throughout the country and interacting directly with the workers. He made himself approachable by having lunch at the dining hall instead of the dining area for executives. When he spoke to people in the company, he made sure to give them his full attention, which made them feel as if they were the only person that mattered in the world. Mullaly also wrote hundreds of hand- written notes to employees in all sections of the company, expressing appreciation and thanking them for their commitment to the company. He is known for having great interpersonal and listening skills, which helped encourage loyalty and motivated the employees to work harder.

Part 2: Emotional Intelligence in Action

Chapter 7 – An Action Plan to Increase Your Emotional Intelligence

Unlike the case of intelligent quotient (IQ), emotional intelligence can be learned and improved. With the proper training, exercise, motivation, and the simple effort of applying what you've learned about emotional intelligence, anyone will be able to raise their emotional quotient (EQ) in order achieve their desired goals. It is similar to learning a particular sport or gaining knowledge on a certain topic. The more we read about the word "motivation," the more we understand its meaning and how it works in people. When we enroll in a course about leadership, we will have at least improved on what we know about it and how we can put it to good use. After playing tennis for a year, we would be much better than we were before picking up the racket for the first time. These are all skills which you can learn and improve on.

We've already discussed why emotional intelligence is useful and the many benefits of having a substantial level of EQ. In this section, we will offer a guide on how you can create an action plan to improve your overall EQ on the most crucial aspects of emotional intelligence. Later on in the final chapter, we will discuss more exercises which you can practice daily to further improve, strengthen, and maintain a healthy level of emotional intelligence in your life.

A good starting point is to get yourself a journal or notebook, specifically for the purpose of helping you build up your emotional intelligence. As you continue reading this book, use the journal to take note of all the points you find the most useful and relevant to you. By then, you should have a rough idea of your own level of EQ. To be more confident of where you stand, you should take an emotional intelligence test. Some suggested EQ test can be found at the end of this chapter. These tests can also help you better understand your strengths and weaknesses, and which areas you need to work on more.

After knowing where you stand in terms of emotional intelligence, you can finalize a list of skills which you want to improve on. You can prioritize skills that you feel you need to improve on urgently and other skills which you can work on at a later time. For example, you can make it a priority to learn the skills you need for your present job or for the job which you are trying to get. You can even try working on easier skills first; you'll increase your chances of success with the easier skills because it will help you gain momentum, motivation, and confidence to move on to more challenging skills later. You should be aware that certain skills have prerequisites, for instance, to manage emotions, you must first be able to understand, identify, and perceive them.

Set up a reasonable timeline or target date for you to achieve your goals. This will help motivate you to be more proactive. Set a shorter timeline for easier skills and a longer timeline for harder skills. These timelines can be changed depending on the situation. You can also create some daily or weekly challenges for yourself if you feel there is an opportunity to work on a particular area due to an event that is taking place around that time.

Once you've figured this out, you can start practicing the skills that you've chosen to work on. This should be practiced in real life situations, such as at school or work. At the same time, you can also engage in role-playing with your family or friends. There's bound to be many real-life opportunities to apply the skills which you are learning, especially in the workplace. For example, if you've been spending most of your time at work lately, you can make it a goal to interact more frequently with your colleagues. You can do so by asking questions or offering to help others with their issues. Be more proactive and take initiatives to work beyond your usual routine. There may even be possible conflicts at work where you can test your skills.

In addition to practicing, it is also important to receive genuine feedback from others. We cannot simply rely on our own judgment and decide if we have made any progress ourselves. You can ask for feedback from someone you are close to and trust. You can also ask for feedback from your superiors at work, it is usually part of their job to give you regular reviews or feedback about your performance at work. Taking the initiative to ask for feedback is also an affirmative action on your part from superiors, as it indicates that you have the desire to improve yourself. This will also give you the chance to practice handling criticism or receiving negative feedback better.

Remember to commit yourself to your action plan and pay attention to your progress. There may be times when you hit a snag or find the particular skill you are working on too difficult. Do not give up so quickly. If a particular skill is difficult, pick different one to work on. You can always return to the difficult skill at another time in the future. Alternatively, you can adjust the timeline to allow more time to work on the difficult skill. Remember to be patient. Developing emotional intelligence may require drastic changes in our behavior, and changing our behavior or attitude which we have adopted for decades will not happen in a mere two or three-week time span. Some people may be able to change easily, but others may not. Everyone is programmed differently, so be patient.

EQ Tests

There are many different tests available that can help you determine your level of emotional intelligence. There are free online tests which are usually simple, and then there are paid tests. These tests are generally more comprehensive and reliable than the free ones.

EQ-i – Emotional Intelligence Inventory

The emotional intelligence inventory is based on a psychometric model which divides emotional intelligence into five sections: self-perception, self-expression, interpersonal, decision-making, and stress management. This is based on the mixed model EQ generally used.

SEI – Six Seconds Emotional Intelligence Test

The SEI test is divided into three categories: know yourself, choose yourself, and give yourself. This test gives a very comprehensive feedback which aims to educate and develop emotional intelligence skills.

GENOS

The Genos test takes into account self-reports as well as reports by superiors or colleagues.

ESCI – Emotional and Social Competency Inventory

This test covers the four components of emotional intelligence by Goleman: awareness of self, awareness of others, management of self, and management of others. This test also requires reporting by other people such as superiors. The ESCI is suitable for people who are considering leadership positions.

MindTools (free test)

This is a short test consisting of 15 questions. Your total score will be tallied, and it will tell you roughly how high your EQ is.

Alpha High IQ Society EQ Test

A 10-question multiple choice test.

Part 3: Discover the Power of Your Own Inner Strength

Chapter 8 – Mastering Self-Awareness

Mastering self-awareness is a crucial first step in improving your emotional intelligence. Without understanding your own emotions, personality, and behavior, it's nearly impossible to communicate effectively with other people.

When you are overcome with emotion, try and take a step back to identify the emotions you are experiencing. Are they positive, negative, or neutral? You can write down the emotions you experience and include the events or circumstance which triggered it. For instance, you may experience dreadful feelings on certain days before heading to work. You may think that it's just the Monday blues. But upon further scrutiny, you find that the reason for this dread has something to do with a meeting you're scheduled to have involving a certain superior in your company. You can dig deeper to find out the exact reason for this dread. It may even be caused by other emotions such as guilt or insecurity.

Understanding how these emotions are triggered and bringing awareness to them is a sign of good emotional intelligence. This can help you manage and regulate your emotions much better. Also, take note of how emotions tend to evolve. For instance, dread may lead to anxiety or distress, and neglect may lead to isolation or fear. There are many ways emotions can be triggered and evolve. It would all depend on each unique circumstances. But most of the time, it is fairly easy to predict the outcome once we understand the nature of these emotions.

Say, for instance, there is a person at work who you don't like. You think to yourself that the reason you dislike them has to do with the way they speak, or how they comb their hair. But they've never actually bothered you in any way. Upon further analysis, you may find that this hatred is actually triggered by something else entirely. Maybe the person that you really like appears to take a liking towards them, and so you realize that this feeling of hate or loathsome is really triggered by jealousy or envy. This might be a difficult pill to swallow for some people, but this is a good thing. We are gaining more awareness about our own emotions, understanding ourselves better, and how emotions work in general. This will help us control our feelings in the future. It will give us the opportunity to improve ourselves, be more mature, and increase in wisdom. When we find that some of these strong emotions we experience were caused by irrational, unreasonable, or childish emotions, we can start to deal with it more logically and rationally. You may soon find that this person you hated is not so bad after all. You begin to see why other people enjoy being around them and you may start liking them yourself or even start a positive and rewarding friendship with them.

Instead of fixing your emotions, learn to recognize them by gaining self-awareness. The goal is to merely identify emotions as they come and to study their dynamics. We can leave time for self-improvement and deeper introspection some other time. When you think that there's an emotion that needs to be fixed, remember that emotions are neither good nor bad. You may sometimes feel the urge to remove certain emotions that you don't feel comfortable having. But you shouldn't look at them that way.

Emotions exist for a reason. For example, most people do not enjoy experiencing fear. Yet, fear performs an essential function in alerting us of a certain danger that requires our immediate attention. Emotions can point us in specific directions which we have to take note of. For instance, we may experience disappointment for not being taken seriously at school or work. If we analyze further into what is causing this emotion, we may find that we simply have not been trying hard enough in performing our tasks. It could also be due to a lack of assertiveness on our part. Therefore, we need to take action and work on improving these areas of our lives. Sometimes, we may be envious of someone and may want to get rid of this emotion. But this simply means that we need to work on improving our self-esteem and confidence. Merely trying to eradicate feelings of disappointment or envy is not the proper approach to take. Look into the root cause that's giving rise to such emotions if you feel strongly enough about it. Emotions help us understand more about ourselves. When we experience despair or sadness, it is sending a signal that we may not be satisfied with something in our life. When we are feeling sorrow, we understand what's important to us. Emotions can give us useful information about our life.

To effectively manage our emotions, it's important to recognize patterns involved whenever an emotion gets triggered. How do we normally react or behave when experiencing certain emotions? For example, a person with anger management issues may be prone to anger which often leads to uncontrollable rage. Under such conditions, they may act very aggressively and cause serious harm to themselves and the people around them. Other people may react to anger differently by bottling it up. Both of these patterns are not desirable and cannot be remedied unless we first become aware of this pattern. After noticing and analyzing this harmful pattern, we can break it by finding better ways to respond. For example, if you are an impulsive person prone to rage, you can train yourself to practice calm deep breathing exercises whenever you sense the rage boiling up. If you tend to bottle up your feelings when you're angry, you can train yourself to express or communicate your feelings in a healthier manner.

We should also pay attention to other physical reactions we experience to certain emotions. For example, when feeling nervous, some people may sweat a lot or their heartbeat will rise, while other people may feel their throat become dry or their muscles stiffen. We can understand more about another person when we understand how emotions work and manifest in our behavior and physical reactions.

Chapter 9 – How to Identify Your Strengths and Weaknesses

Part of raising our self-awareness involves knowing and understanding our own strengths and weaknesses. We may already have an idea of what they are. Identifying our own weaknesses may not be as easy as learning about our strengths, but it will become easier when we learn to analyze our emotions from an objective standpoint.

Understanding our strengths and weaknesses will help us make better decisions. It will also allow us to take action in leveraging our strengths to produce the desired outcome, and know how to keep our weaknesses from getting in the way. In addition to performing an analysis on ourselves, it would also be beneficial to seek feedback from someone we trust and ask for their opinion on the matter. There are many different personalities or psychological evaluations which we can take to help us better understand our own strengths, such as the Core Values Index, VIA Character Strengths Assessment, or DiSC test.

Journaling would be a good place to start. Ideas and thoughts may appear at random places when they are least expected, so having a journal can help us note them down as they occur. It may come out all of a sudden on a busy day at work. By quickly noting it down in a journal, we can come back to it at a less hectic time; otherwise, we may forget about it completely.

In addition to writing down our strengths and weaknesses, we can also note all the thoughts and emotions we are experiencing as part of the self-awareness process and learn to understand all the various emotions and their dynamics. We can categorize our strengths and weaknesses by the different roles we perform. These roles could be as an employee, superior, subordinate, agent, mentor, parent, sibling, student, or spouse. There may be certain weaknesses that you've identified as a husband, such as being emotionally unavailable to your spouse in times of difficulty. As a student, you may be very quiet during class due to shyness even though you have a lot of great ideas to share with the class. It might be the case that you may have no weaknesses in a particular role such as a worker, but many weaknesses in other roles such as a parent.

By identifying our weaknesses, we can give ourselves the opportunity for self-improvement. We can set goals as to which abilities we may want to improve to fulfill the individual roles we play at home or work. For instance, you may be particularly weak at motivating people, but you'll never be able to improve on this factor if you're not aware of it in the first place. Once we gain awareness, we can take steps to improve ourselves by finding out more about it through reading and learning.

Chapter 10 – How to Improve Motivation, Avoid Procrastination and Distractions

Another component of emotional intelligence is motivation. Having motivation simply means having a sense of enthusiasm in living our lives and in specific activities in which we occupy. This enthusiasm is derived from the desire to achieve our goals and it's what drives us forward to fulfill that goal.

According to Goleman, there are four components of motivation: achievement driven, commitment, ambition, and optimism. Motivation can be in the form of intrinsic or extrinsic. Intrinsic motivation refers to motivation that comes from the desires within us, such as sincerely wanting to improve ourselves, performing or participating in an activity because we really enjoy doing it, or creating something because we find it personally fulfilling or rewarding.

Extrinsic motivation occurs when we are motivated to perform an activity due to some external reward or to avoid some kind of penalty. These external factors can be in the form of money, promotion, or prize, or to avoid losing our jobs, getting bad grades in school, or getting a ticket for speeding. The dynamics of intrinsic and extrinsic motivations work differently depending on the circumstances, and in terms of improving our emotional intelligence, there is a preference to have more intrinsic motivation as it will carry a more wholesome effect and feel more rewarding. Extrinsic motivation can be useful when there is a task that has to be completed which is particularly unexciting, unpleasant, or boring. However, it can hurt a person's motivation when they already enjoy doing the task. Understanding how motivation works is an important skill to have for people in a leadership position such as supervisors, team leaders, and managers.

The motivation level in our psyche is not always constant and tends to fluctuate depending on the situations we find ourselves in. Therefore, there is a need to constantly keep our motivation in check and learn ways to re-motivate ourselves whenever we're feeling lazy.

One of the basic things needed to improve motivation is to set the correct kind of goals. Whether it is an intrinsic or extrinsic oriented goal, we need to make sure that it's not too small. Setting appropriate goals has to be done with care, and there are plenty of strategies available on how to set the best kind of goals. An example of a correct goal setting strategy we can adopt is the SMART goal setting method. SMART is an acronym which suggests that goals should be Specific, Measurable, Attainable, Realistic, and Timely. There are other theories which suggest that setting unrealistic goals can also lead to positive results.

Developing a love for learning new things can also boost or maintain our motivation levels. This works out in the favor of people who are naturally curious about how things work. For others, there are plenty of ways to foster a love of learning, such as taking on new challenges, cultivating an interest in new artistic expressions, or having more activities which stimulate curiosity, such as reading or exploring.

We can decide to learn a new skill or language that we have a keen interest in, even if it's not relevant to our desired work. This will most certainly help increase our motivation in general. For example, in this age of big data, where more and more data is becoming available, there's a good reason to learn more about how we can manage it, or use data mining tools to find useful information about work related projects. We can also learn a new language simply because we love that language, or a large number of our clients speak it, which would help us create a better relationship with them if we can communicate in their native language.

Being around motivated people can also help us maintain our motivation. When we hang around like-minded motivated individuals, we will continually inspire others to be motivated and reach for their goals.

Finding intrinsic motivation can be difficult for some people because they may not have developed sufficient self-awareness. But once they understand themselves better, it is easy to find where their passions lie. The effectiveness of intrinsic motivations cannot be understated and its results are always deeply rewarding and satisfying.

How to Avoid Procrastination

To maintain a healthy level of motivation, you need to know how to avoid procrastination and minimize distractions. Procrastination occurs when you avoid or delay doing tasks you are supposed to complete — for example, creating an action plan to improve your emotional intelligence level. You are supposed to get a notebook to record all the relevant details and observations regarding this goal, but up to now, you still have not attempted to find one. Or it could be that you were supposed to take a certification exam for a particular software, which could help boost your chances of getting the job you want. However, you still have not registered or studied for the exam.

There are three possible reasons why people tend to put things off and procrastinate. The first possibility is that the person is a perfectionist. People who fall in this category tend to want everything done in perfect order and harmony. Any slight issue or imperfection in their work may cause irrational anxiety and stress. Therefore, instead of working to eradicate this flaw, they will procrastinate and delay any eventual error.

Another reason people procrastinate is due to the fear of failure. When the fear of failing is strong enough, people will use up any opportunity they have to procrastinate and leave the task until they have just enough time to complete it. Putting it off until the very last minute also fulfills another psychological purpose which the procrastinator may not be aware of; it gives them an excuse in case they fail. This kind of action is often described as self-sabotage or self-handicap, which is sometimes actuated by the subconscious mind.

The third reason people procrastinate is due to the fear of success or the unknown. Success in any particular endeavor will often lead to bigger responsibilities and expectations. They may not be ready for their lives to change, even if it leads to better opportunities. People in this category may be talented but lack motivation, uncertain of what they want in life. Self-sabotage may also play a role here because the person might think that they're not worthy of experiencing higher levels of success.

Whatever the reason for procrastination may be, it will always lead to bigger problems. Besides the obvious that the work we put will be sub-optimal, procrastination can cause more profound stress, regret, and possibly even depression.

It is worth noting that there are healthy forms of procrastination as opposed to the destructive forms that we discussed. Healthy procrastination occurs when we leave things to the last minute intentionally to build pressure and motivation to get certain work done. It can help us work faster and make us focus better due to the time constraint.

To overcome procrastination, we need to reprogram our minds from thinking that we "have to" finish a task to we "want to" get it done. Whenever we feel that there is a task that we have no choice but to do, it makes us feel disempowered and may cause us to resort to self-sabotage. But if we change the phrasing to one which suggests that we genuinely want to do a task for the sake of it, it makes us feel more in control over the matter. Another way to change our thinking is to do the unpleasant task first. You can also implement a reward mechanism when you complete certain tasks, such as a special meal that you have been craving for weeks or by treating yourself to the spa.

Self-sabotage

If you believe that you are prone to sabotaging yourself in your quest for success, try to understand this notion deeper. That way, you can fix this problem sooner rather than barking up the wrong tree and getting nothing resolved. The first step is to understand what the symptoms of self-sabotage are, what causes people to self-sabotage, and how to overcome it. Most of the time, people who engage in self-sabotage do so without realizing it because it involves the subconscious mind. Ways that people self-sabotage and the signs to look out for include procrastination, isolation, overeating, taking drugs or alcohol, and engaging in other non-productive or harmful activities.

There are various reasons why people self-sabotage. The most common is a lack of self-esteem. When people lack self- confidence, they subconsciously blow their chances of success because they believe that their not worthy of it. This is closely related to the imposter syndrome, where people feel like frauds and have an irrational fear of being exposed when they come close to achieving any degree of success. Another reason people self-sabotage is to create a convenient scapegoat in case of failure or rejection. For example, when you leave tasks to the very last minute, perhaps semi-subconsciously, when the resulting work is poor, you'll have a good reason for failing. Or when you become argumentative or demanding with your partner without reason, and they leave you, you have a handy explanation to soften the blow. Because it might hurt less when you fail after not trying hard enough rather than giving your best, you self-sabotage. You may have also fully subscribed to the mantra: Better the devil you know than the devil you don't.

To overcome self-sabotage, you must first acknowledge this behavior. You need to get to the root of the problem instead of merely trying to fix the symptoms. Understand what is driving this self-sabotaging behavior. It is often a case of misguided self-protection, where our subconscious or ego believes that it is shielding us from danger. When you understand your fears, it makes it easier to tackle the problem and convince yourself that the fear is unfounded. Try and find familiar patterns of self- sabotage in your life. It could be something you do at work or in your relationship. Find it and get to the root of the problem. By getting familiar with the pattern, you can catch yourself the next time you're about to engage in self-sabotaging behavior.

Distractions

As you embark on this journey towards self-transformation, there can be many distractions that come along the way, causing you to lose focus. It can be a phone call from your brother, a text message from your colleague, or an eye- catching advertisement showing up in the internet browser. You may be in the middle of writing a report when you get a text notification from an ex-colleague. It was nothing remarkable, just a funny meme. But it was indeed funny otherwise she wouldn't have sent it to you. You laugh, then automatically decide to check for any other messages you've received. One thing leads to another, and now are scrolling through Twitter and Facebook feeds. It is all fun and light-hearted, but by the time you get back to work maybe 30 minutes later, you lose focus, and your motivation is down the toilet. Now you need to start all over again and build your momentum back from scratch.

We often overlook the impact of distractions and seldom prepare ourselves sufficiently to overcome them. We were never taught in school or at home how to stay focused and avoid distractions along the way. Dealing with distraction is not easy, but there are methods we can use to minimize its effects to stay on track with our duties. Besides losing concentration, a study found that even a minor distraction can cause people to make more than twice the amount of mistakes in their work than if they had not been distracted. Distractions can also be long term. For instance, you may find social activities to engage in with your friends, such as partying, dining, or sports. While some of these activities can be beneficial for your wellbeing, others can be a distraction to some of your long-term goals and aspirations, such as finding a new job or trying to improve your EQ.

One of the first things you can do to combat distraction is to recognize them as they come. Some people may not be aware of distractions, accepting them as if they are part of life. Although we'll never be able to eliminate them completely, we can take steps to minimize and manage them the right way.

Learn to be aware of distractions as they come and understand how they're impacting your work. Once you are aware of these distractions, you can tackle them head-on.

One of the main sources of distractions nowadays is our smartphones. Most of our phones readily enable notifications by default. The majority of these notifications are unimportant. So the first step is to take control of your phone instead of letting it control you. Make it distract-proof. If you own other potentially distracting devices, rein them in as well. Switch off notifications for non-essential items like messaging and social media apps on your phone. If you use a particular messaging app for both work and leisure, for example, Whatsapp or Skype, switch off notifications for the non-work-related group chats. There may be apps that cannot be configured to disable notifications; in this case, it's better to delete it completely from your phone.

Setting a deadline for a particular task can help you focus on your work. However, creating a deadline specifically for this purpose may not be so easy to follow, especially if you have plenty of time beyond this deadline to accomplish your work. Therefore when creating deadlines, you must make it abuse- proof. Make the time constraint slightly shorter than the actual due date. When you realize that you have a short amount of time, it will help you work faster and ignore distractions easier as they come your way. When you create a deadline for a certain project, it's beneficial to have another task lined up right after. This way, you'll know that you can't delay the work as you have other tasks waiting to be completed later.

Find the best time to do your work, like when you expect to have the least amount of distractions. For example, if you have children and plan to work at home, find a time when your children are most likely to be occupied with their own activities and avoid doing work when they require your attention. It can be after they are asleep or when they are doing homework.

While it's easy to remember short term tasks, it can be harder to remember longer-term goals. Therefore, keeping your goals in mind will help you focus and raise your awareness of the distractions that you need to evade. The longer you go about not affirming your goals, the more likelier you'll be distracted.

Overcoming internal distractions will be a bit trickier. These are the distracting thoughts in your mind. More often than not, it makes your mind wander off without being consciously aware of it. Setting a tight deadline as mentioned previously can also help you overcome these distractions. You can also try and create a dedicated work station if you need to get work done from home. When you create a proper work station, and you associate it with the purpose of solely doing work, chores, and other non-leisure activities, it can help put you in the right mindset to do interruption-free work. You can also work on creating an ergonomic workspace at home or in the office to minimize unnecessary distraction resulting from minor inconveniences or discomforts. For example, having a suitable work chair can make you comfortable while working and reduce the need to stretch or move around.

Learning how to build and manage momentum can also help make the most of your time to get work done faster. Momentum is a psychological state of performing a particular task when we are completely focused, with ideas pouring in and moving at a brisk pace. Avoid taking breaks when you feel that solid momentum going on. When you are just getting started or feel that things are going too slow, work on building momentum. It doesn't usually arrive all of a sudden; it has to build up slowly. You can kickstart it by working on smaller or easier tasks first. Planning your work, such as creating an outline or a mind map of how you want to complete the task can help reduce distraction when moving from one section of your work to the next.

Positive distraction

It's worth noting that distractions can be used positively. Whenever we are reacting emotionally towards something and need to maintain a calm demeanor, we can use a distraction to divert our thoughts away from the triggering event. By doing this, we can control and manage our emotions better. You can also use positive distractions to break someone's influence. For example, a manipulator may be trying to influence you using various techniques such as flattery or criticism to maintain control over you. You can use a positive distraction to divert yourself from the situation that's keeping you under their influence. To distract yourself successfully, you first need to realize what you are experiencing. Once you recognize your emotional state and your need to snap out of it, try and distract yourself by simply looking around you. Find something to look at and think about what it is, why it's there, what's the meaning of it, and why it is designed in such a way. Distracting yourself helps you move out of the emotional zone, buys you some time, and helps you deal with the situation calmly with a stable mind.

Chapter 11 – The Importance of Confidence and How to Increase It

Self-confidence is a fundamental aspects of emotional intelligence. Confidence can be defined as the state self- assurance we have of our own abilities and how our behavior conveys it to the world. Self-confidence is often used interchangeably with self-esteem; however, the concepts are not the same. Self-confidence is concerned with having an appreciation of our abilities, while self-esteem is more concerned about our own self-worth, self-respect, and self-love. But the two concepts are connected, and often self-confidence can help increase self-esteem and vice versa. To build up emotional intelligence, we will focus on how we can increase self-confidence and keep our self-esteem in check, maintaining it at a healthy level.

Having confidence can be distinguished with having low self- esteem. People with little confidence may not believe in their own abilities or are afraid to acknowledge it. Sometimes, they may even down-play their abilities due to low self-esteem or because they do not want people to put such high expectations on them. This state of mind often gives rise to what people are recently calling the imposter syndrome. People with imposter syndrome often believe that they do not deserve to achieve success because they doubt their own capabilities despite the clear evidence of their competencies. They often have an irrational fear of being exposed as a fraud by their peers. Whenever something good may come their way, they feel that they don't deserve it or that it was due to sheer luck.

Too much confidence occurs when an individual overestimates their own capability. Overconfident people tend to think they're better at certain skills than they really are. Overconfidence can often result in catastrophic disasters on a larger scale and major problems for the person with such a mindset. There is a real risk for people to fall into the trap of being overconfident, so it's important to steer clear of it. When we overestimate our own abilities and value, we open ourselves up to the risk of losing time, trust, or money. This brings us back to why it's important to develop deeper self-awareness, to understand our own strengths and limitations.

Therefore, the first part of having confidence is knowing and understanding exactly the true nature of our own abilities to not underestimate or overestimate them. The second part is correctly conveying or communicating our true abilities to people around us.

Confidence is important if we want to achieve success in our career. Confidence can ensure success at work because when we exude confidence, we are conveying to others that we are capable of handling all the requirements demanded of us. For example, take a junior data analyst in a media company who desires to be in a senior or supervisory position. The position will certainly involve more responsibilities, independence, and accountability, among other things.

The person who wishes to be promoted to such positions must have all these qualities to be considered for it. If for instance, the person does possess all the required skills for the job, he or she must be able to prove it. They need to inspire confidence in the decision makers' mind. Self-confidence can be expressed and manifested through our words, action, or body language. Having confidence assures the decision makers that this person is indeed capable and deserves to get the promotion.

Confidence is also important in school. A study found a correlation between confident students in elementary school and success later in life.

If you have children, it is essential to teach them self- confidence at a young age. The parents must help their children gain confidence at home. Of course, to teach them self-confidence effectively, the parents need to possess this trait themselves. It would be impossible to teach someone something we don't already have. This healthy nurturing process with children begins at home.

There are many ways in which we can build self-confidence. It's better to work in increasing our confidence after we've developed sufficient self-awareness of our own strengths and weakness.

Leave your comfort zone

People with low self-confidence tend to be afraid of realizing their true potential because of the fear of failure or refection. They often stay in their comfort zone and perform less demanding and challenging work. In this situation, it is difficult to grow their confidence to a healthy level because they never get the opportunity to confirm and assure themselves of what their true potential is. If you are suffering from low confidence or low self-esteem, it is necessary to leave your comfort zone. Leave your comfort zone regularly or as often as you can. The more frequently, the better.

The important thing to remember when leaving your comfort zone is not to expect to encounter success every time. There is a reason why it's called "leaving the comfort zone." The point of this exercise is to get used to being uncomfortable. To help us overcome our fear of failure, rejection, or even success. Once we overcome these fears, we can then truly examine where our abilities lie by consistently testing ourselves with real-life problems and gauging more accurately what we are truly capable of. It can help us confirm what we already speculated, or dismiss it and force us to reevaluate our abilities to more appropriate levels. Whatever the outcome, we can be certain of ourselves in the future. Never be discouraged by failures. There may be many factors involved such as luck simply not being on your side that day. You must understand that you have nothing to lose with leaving your comfort zone and everything to gain.

Face your fear of rejection

Overcoming a fear of rejection is actually not as hard as it seems. The secret to overcoming this fear is to learn how to handle your emotions when faced with it. Just like everything else, like learning tennis or getting better at cooking, it takes practice and getting used to. There is no denying how painful it is to get rejected, especially if it involves something that you really wanted, such as your dream job or your school of choice. There are many reasons why some people can take rejection better than others. It could be because they have been pampered from a young age to always get what they wanted even if undeserved. The key to handling rejections better is first to desensitize yourself from it. You should always take action to pursue your goals, and a fear of rejection will always hold you back. This is one of the reasons why people tend to stay in their comfort zones and stagnate for prolonged periods. The more times we get rejected, the easier it becomes to handle it. A fun way to overcome this is to try the 100 days of rejection challenge popularize by Jia Jiang, where you make an outrageous proposal to random people in order to be rejected. You can also try making genuine requests just to get used to rejections. The results will be remarkable.

Learn to dress better

When you dress the way you want people to see you, it can have a dramatic effect on your self-confidence. Learn to dress better by observing people you admire. Every detail of your clothing can help make a big difference, from your shoes, shirt, blazer, glasses, and even non-visible accessories such as your underwear and perfume. Dressing well enables you to feel better and helps minimize any doubts you may have.

Work out

Working out or exercising can have a positive effect on your overall confidence. We already know how exercising can help us maintain a healthy body, but it can also have a positive effect on our mental health. Working out helps the body release endorphins which make people feel good about themselves. It can also have longer-lasting effects on our mental health and reduce instances of depression and anxiety. A study published in 2000 found evidence that working out regularly is a very effective way of increasing a person's self-confidence. Therefore, try and make a long-term goal to incorporate routine work out sessions in your life. Pick an exercise that you enjoy and try to stick to it like any other commitments you have. Whenever you feel like you are losing interest in a particular workout, try doing different variations of it or move on to a new exercise altogether. The key is to maintain a workout routine. You have a choice to do light or heavy workouts depending on your preference. Some forms of exercise you can try include weightlifting, CrossFit, yoga, running, jogging, strolling, home workouts, or regular sports activities.

Stop competing with other people

Comparing yourself to other people exposes you to feelings of envy, which hurts your confidence. If you find that the people you're comparing yourself with are doing much better in life better than you, it lowers your self-esteem. It is common for people to compare with others how they fare in terms of earnings, possessions, or achievements. Even if you are leading the race, such practice should be avoided at all costs. It is worthwhile to remember that life is not a competition; everyone should be going after their own goals and competing with themselves to become the best version of themselves. Every person has their own stories and circumstances, and each with their own sets of privileges, advantages, and disadvantages. Therefore, avoid competing with others and focus on your individual needs and goals.

Enjoying this book so far? I'd love it for you to share your thoughts and post a quick review on Amazon!

To leave a review, go to: **ReviewEQ.com**

Part 4: Self-Management: How to Control Your Emotions

Chapter 12 – How to Manage and Conquer Out-of-Control Emotions

You've heard the saying "action speaks louder than words." This is true, but only if we are comparing words with actions, as words must always precede action. Without saying anything, nobody can expect an action to be carried out. For lack of a better term, words are pretty much as important as the action it entails. They have the power to heal and hurt. The way we use our words will play a crucial role in how other people receive the message. If we have a severe lack of tactfulness, any non- malicious words we speak can be taken the wrong way by the recipient.

A good example would be when we ask someone for a favor. The absence of the word "please" has the potential to make a straightforward matter into an unnecessary full-blown war between siblings. Sometimes, people may detect a certain tone which they do not appreciate. Being able to structure our words in a way which the recipient can receive the message in the best possible manner is one of the key indicators of superior emotional intelligence. Therefore, it is important to always think things through before speaking. This is especially true whenever our minds are under the influence of certain emotions.

On the other hand, some words have the potential to heal and change the lives of others. In any case, we could help someone out tremendously with some simple kind words, but often, we only manage to say things without making any impact. Our words have the potential to heal, soothe, motivate, and make other people feel like a family. This is part of how we can develop good communication skills. We should always consider the effect our words can have on the people we speak to. And the way we do this is by not allowing our emotions to speak on our behalf. Always take the time to consider what you should say to elicit the best response you desire in the person you're speaking with. Emotionally intelligent people will speak mindfully with compassion. They will also listen attentively to what the other person is saying. Our words can be used to empower and influence people to be better.

Whenever you feel particularly good about something, it's advisable not to make important decisions. Being happy is also an emotional state which may cloud your rational thought process. This excited state may make you feel optimistic about everything you encounter, which can influence your thinking in a way that foregoes any rational thought. For example, there may be a particular project being offered to your company which could be a very poorly conceived idea destined for failure. But being in such a happy and optimistic mood, you may be tempted or easily convinced to accept it without giving it enough assessment. It may be easier to remember not to make decisions when in a bad mood, but it might be challenging when you find yourself in a positive mood.

Chapter 13 – Expressing Healthy Emotions

Human beings will experience many different emotions on any given day. They may be positive emotions such as delight or compassion, or negative emotions such as anger or sadness. These emotions may be expressed in many different ways; sometimes they can be controlled, sometimes they cannot. The magnitude of these emotions may also vary depending on the situations. The higher the magnitude of the emotion, the more difficult it is to control it. For example, it's easier to control your excitement if you win $50 in the lottery compared to if you win $50 million. If you were eating alone at a food court downtown when suddenly someone tapped you on your shoulder, you might experience a little fright if you were not expecting to meet anyone. However, if you were at home alone and someone suddenly tapped you on your shoulder, the fright will be much greater, causing your heartbeat to race.

This is merely an example, but what we have to keep in mind is that emotions should always be expressed healthily. As we grow older, we tend to control our emotions, both positive and negative, according to societal standards. This is good because we all need to control certain emotions, especially when we are out with other people. But at the same time, bottling up emotions can lead to undesired results. Therefore, a delicate balance is needed. Emotionally intelligent people can balance this effectively and understand when to control emotions and when to express them.

Most of the time, it's the negative emotions that need to be controlled. Everybody wants to be happy, and nobody enjoys being sad. So, we normally share happiness and keep sadness to ourselves. There are times, however, when positive emotions should be controlled. For example, your boss just gave you a compliment for a job that you placed a considerable amount of effort into, and you're feeling very cheerful at work; you decide to talk to your colleague, who unfortunately was just reprimanded by his boss. In this case, it would be wise to suppress your joy a little. Most of the time, people do not express their emotions outwardly, so it takes a bit more effort and some EQ skills to read hidden emotions.

Expressing healthy emotions has to be made at the appropriate time and place. As for negative emotions, while we often have to control it when we are with other people, these emotions still need to be expressed one way or another.

Chapter 14 – How to Control Anger and Use It in a Positive Way

Emotionally intelligent people would not allow their emotions to influence crucial decisions that they need to make. Any important decision may affect not only yourself but also the people around you such as your children, subordinates, or your company. These decisions generally require a thorough, logical analysis before they can be made. Becoming emotional will make it difficult for you to think rationally concerning a particular issue. For example, feeling angry or hopeless about a situation causes you to react emotionally, which will almost always be lacking in proper reasoning.

A complex issue can be solved if the person responsible for that issue took into account every factor involved and used proper reasoning and intuition. But if they allow their emotions to dictate their decisions, it will rarely end well because many key elements are not being appropriately considered. Whenever people are facing a crisis, all their cognitive faculties fall into a haze, making it difficult to function at an optimum level. These negative emotions tend to snowball into something bigger, which may cause you to start seeing everything negatively and be filled with a lot of resentment and negativity.

Being angry is probably the worse state of emotion to be in when making tough decisions. Anger can impair your rational thought and cognitive control. Whenever you feel a strong emotion such as anger or a sense of hopelessness, avoid making any big decisions. If an action for a particularly important issue is required or scheduled during such a period, try and postpone it to a later date or time. Try and regain your composure first before returning to the issue.

Usually, all we need is a little bit of time to calm down. Time will often help bring negative emotions down a notch. When your emotions are down to a manageable level, you can then allow your rational mind to find answers and make the appropriate decision.

Chapter 15 – How to React to Tough Situations with Resilience

Throughout your life, you will always be faced with difficulty. It has been this way since the dawn of humanity. There may be days when challenges become much harder than usual and days which are a lot better than normal. We will always try and minimize difficult days and maximize positive days with notable degrees of success as we gain more knowledge and expertise about certain things. But it is almost impossible to eliminate tough situations in our life completely. The problem we face is that as we succeed in reducing the incidence of the issues in our lives, we acclimate to continued success with minimal interruptions, causing us to become more sensitized to troubles as they come. The effects can be quite damaging if we cannot handle it properly with resilience and bounce back on the right track. Therefore, there is a need to be prepared for times when troubles strike.

A good starting point for dealing with difficult situations is to learn how to accept it as an opportunity to learn and grow. Dealing with problems that we've never anticipated before benefits us as we learn to overcome them. Strong character is built by overcoming strong resistance we face in life. Dormant parts of our mind and body become stimulated by certain problems we face, causing our bodies to release stress hormones such as cortisol and adrenaline to help us deal with the situation. Studies found that short bursts of stress hormones are actually good for the mind and the body. Just like everything else though, having too little or too much stress can lead to serious problems.

So how do we deal with tough situations? Remember that any event which is not life-threatening cannot cause prolonged stress without us allowing it to be as such. Most of the time, we're the ones making the problem bigger than it actually is. It's not the stress hormones that are causing us problems; rather, it's our attitude towards stress. An emotionally intelligent person would be aware of this situation and skilled at handling it correctly. Becoming self-aware during times of trouble is an essential first step in helping us deal with the issue. Once we become aware, only then can we manage our emotions towards recovery as efficiently and quickly as possible.

Chapter 16 – How to Free Yourself from Other People's Opinions and Judgment

Since we were children, we've been taught to behave ourselves in public around other people. It's common sense not to disrupt others in the cinema or run around the shopping mall, but sometimes, our parents may just be embarrassed by our actions even though such behavior is perfectly normal for children. As we grow older and our ego develops, we want to be appreciated, validated, or admired by people who we want to impress. It could be our talent, skills in playing a sport, our sick dance moves, quick intelligence, pretty face or buffed up bod. Many times, we continue this pattern into adulthood by having nice cars, expensive suits, and sky-high earnings.

A problem develops when we rely too much on what other people think about us and tailor our lives to fit other people's expectations. Sometimes, these expectations that we think other people have may not even be real and could merely be our own false projection. When we allow other people's opinion to matter more than our own, our life becomes a mere fantasy, or an elaborate play, acted out for an audience. But this is only the beginning. The real problem occurs when life does not play out the way you intended. For example, your spouse seeking a divorce, your business going bankrupt, mounting unreasonable debts, etc. When faced with such situations, the correct response is to find ways to overcome it, but if you care too much about other people's judgment, then you'll get distracted from doing what is necessary. Instead of solving the problem, you'll be more invested with covering up your failures.

Some people may think that relying on other people's opinion gives them greater motivation to reach for goals they may not have even thought of. Adopting goals inspired by other people is okay. But it should end there. When people inspire us to reach certain goals, it should be adopted as our own only if we want it ourselves. Therefore, ask yourself if such a goal is really what you want. And if the answer is yes, then go for it. Reach for that goal because you want it. Do not make the mistake of adopting it to impress the others.

Some people may have fallen deeply into this trap, requiring more effort to break free of it. Still, there are others who may not have fallen so deeply and are living their best life by not caring about what other people think about them. There are several things to remember if you want to learn to free yourself from other people's judgment.

Know yourself

By gaining higher self-awareness, we can rediscover our true self. We can start by sifting out all the distractions and noise to understand ourselves better. When we get in touch with our true selves, we recognize our wants, needs, and desires, free from the opinions of others. Without knowing yourself, it is difficult to know what you truly want and formulate clear goals. This may cause you to fall back to living your life through the lens of other people. When you know what you want, it makes it easier to focus on things that matter.

You can't please everyone.

Don't expect to please everyone. Ideally, you should only aim to please yourself and people who really matter such as your children, partner, parents, or friends. There will always be people who dislike you. Why should you care? As long as you are living your own life the way you want, nothing else should matter. If it's really bothering you that much, try and do a quick analysis of whether you have done something wrong with your life. If you found something, then obviously you need to fix it. But if you can't find anything wrong, then clearly the problem is with them and not you.

What goes around comes around

The more we judge other people, the more we care what others think about us. The less we judge them, the less we care what they think.

Stop overthinking

Overthinking simply means what it says. You're thinking about a situation more than necessary, which is always pointless. Overthinking usually involves the thought of being judged harshly when that's often not the case. It can also mean that you are indeed being judged, but you're unnecessarily playing it out in your head, again and again, torturing yourself for no good reason. Overthinking can lead to finding creative ways to pull yourself further down by creating a chain of negative events from a negative thought. It is easy to recognize when you are overthinking. Whenever you find yourself feeling down and thinking about a situation too much, there is a high chance that you are overthinking. Catch yourself the next time it occurs and remind yourself how pointless this is, and start replacing those negative thoughts with more positivity.

Mind your own business

You need to stop assuming or asking people what they think about you. Whatever they think isn't really any of your business. If you are worried about the negative thoughts they might have about you, then the chances are that they're negative people who you don't want to associate with.

Try to be less sensitive

It could be the case that you are being too sensitive towards what other people say about you. This can take a lot of precious energy when you could have used it in doing something more productive. Try and desensitize your triggers by developing a thick skin and think about how to regain all that lost energy spent on something as useless as poring over opinions of people who don't even matter.

YOLO

Life is truly very short, and we only get one shot at it. Is it worth your time living life vicariously through people who do not matter? Try and live your own life. Savor life for yourself and enjoy every minute of it.

Chapter 17 – How to Deal with Criticism

Most people do not enjoy receiving criticisms. But this is something that we need to expect in life, especially in the professional environment. Learning to accept criticism is a sign of high emotional intelligence, self-confidence, and maturity. To deal with criticisms effectively, we need to understand the nature of such criticisms. We know that some are positive and genuine, which are meant to be constructive. These types of criticism are delicate and need to be delivered with care to not be taken the wrong way by the recipient. We know that this is not an easy task unless the person giving that criticism has a decent amount of emotional intelligence (Providing tactful criticism will be covered separately in this chapter). There are also criticisms which are ingenuine. These may come from people with malicious intent who just want to take the opportunity to put you down and demoralize you. Understanding the context and what kind of criticism we are getting will help us deal with it more effectively.

Here are some of the things we can consider when dealing with criticisms:

1. <u>What is the context?</u> Was the criticism given at work, school, or home? What was the criticism related to? Could it be something you wrote in a report or email? Could it be related to something outside of work? Considering the context of the criticism will guide you on how you can respond to it.

2. <u>The person who is giving the criticism.</u> It is equally important to take note of your relationship to the person who is giving the criticism. It could be coming from your superior, parent, boss, or it could be from a colleague or a friend. Quite clearly, you should take criticism from your superior more seriously than someone who is on the same level as you. That is not to say that you should simply brush off criticisms from your colleagues or friends. They need to be respected and given due

consideration too, especially when such criticism was not made maliciously.

3. <u>Put aside your emotions.</u> Before analyzing the criticism deeper, we need to first put aside our emotions. Do not feel bad about being down when getting criticized. No one likes criticism. Therefore, you are not alone. How you react and respond to criticism is what makes a difference. If you are feeling particularly bad because of a critique and cannot seem to get over it, it could be a sign of low self-confidence. Try and work on improving your confidence and you will undoubtedly be able to handle criticism better. You can also try and think about the criticism as being directed at someone else.

4. <u>What was the criticism about?</u> This is where we go to the crux of the issue. After putting aside our emotions, we should be in a better position to analyze the criticism objectively. This is to avoid any flawed judgment we may have about the person's intention when they gave the criticism. Analyze the criticism from a neutral standpoint. Think about whether it was deserved. If you feel that it wasn't, then it may be because it was ingenuine, or it could be a mistake on the part of the person criticizing. Depending on the situation, it would be a good idea to seek further clarification from them or try to explain to them why you think the criticism was not warranted. If you did not deserve to be criticized, then you shouldn't simply let it go. Try and think about the intention and intended effect behind such criticism. If you accept it and follow the implicit recommendations, will it actually be better? If yes, then there you have it. It is no longer criticism, but a piece of advice on how to become better. Accept it as a gift and thank the person for such valuable feedback. Most of the time, we receive negative feedback because of something we truly deserved. If you still feel particularly bad in spite of that, then you really need to work on finding the root cause. It could be an issue relating to your self-esteem, self-confidence, ego, or upbringing. Try and pinpoint the

cause of it and surely there will be room for improvement.

5. <u>How to deal with malicious criticism.</u> Sometimes we may encounter situations where people give criticism maliciously in order to undermine us. It could be coming from a colleague who is particularly overcompetitive, or an insecure superior. We can normally deduce this by looking at the surrounding circumstances. Usually, you can ignore such malicious criticism. It is quite pointless to expend further energy on it if it will not help you improve. But if the problem persists and has become a regular occurrence at the workplace, then this may be a sign that this company's environment is toxic, and it's probably in your best interest to work elsewhere.

6. <u>Admit your mistake.</u> Once we have analyzed the criticism objectively and found that it was indeed warranted and not made maliciously, we need to accept and admit our mistake. This is another difficult part of the process. Some people may find it to be an easier task, but most will find admitting their mistakes to be very difficult. There are some who may even avoid doing so by finding excuses, lying, or putting the blame on someone else. There are those who may issue a letter of apology followed by a statement indicating that they are anything but sorry. Any difficulty we may have in admitting our mistakes may be caused by the same reasons why some people find it hard to accept criticism, such as a lack of confidence or self-esteem. We may think that admitting our mistake is a sign of weakness, but the opposite is true. It shows that you are not afraid to face further scrutiny for your mistake and that you're not concerned about people having doubts in your abilities as a result, because you know for sure that you have learned from your mistakes and will not repeat it again in the future. The truth is that admitting our own mistakes is a sign of courage, integrity, and self-confidence. If you are in a leadership position, it becomes even more crucial to admit your

mistakes because you need to set an example to your subordinates, which will improve their trust and respect for you.

7. <u>Move on.</u> Once you have accepted the criticism and admitted your mistakes, you will learn from them. If necessary, you can take additional steps to prevent yourself and others from making the same mistake in the future by suggesting new procedures or adding new steps to existing processes to avoid future occurrences.

Part 5: How to Connect with Others and Improve Relationships

Chapter 18 – How to Understand and Connect with Others on a Deeper Level

We connect with people by building relationships with them. Just like penguins, wolves, or elephants, humans depend on building relationships and connecting with one another to feel complete. There are many types of relationships we can build with the people around us such as friendship, romance, professional, or a combination of different types of relationships. Some relationships are strong and long-lasting, while others are casual or fleeting.

Professional relationship

We build professional relationships with people who work in the same environment as us. These relationships exist solely because we've been hired by the same company to perform specific duties and fulfill certain organizational goals together. Therefore, we build professional relationships with the people who work closely with us such as our teammates and superiors. Most of us spend more time with the people we work with; therefore, it is only prudent to build healthy relationships with them. It is often the case that people develop friendships at work. Professional relationships also exist outside of organizations with people we regularly encounter, such as our clients, customers, agents, suppliers, and others who work in the same industry. Building professional relationships with the people outside of your organization is always beneficial, as it can help you gain a better understanding of where you stand, widen your horizon, and make you more visible and recognizable.

Friendship

We can build friendships with any person we regularly encounter in life. Children often develop friendships with one another in the same school and bonds tend to grow among people in the workplace. The ability to understand the difference between professional and friendly relations, and when and where to draw the line is a skill which requires a healthy amount of emotional intelligence. Friendships are based on mutual interest, trust, and affection. Some people place more importance on friendships than family relations.

Family relations

We build family relationships with our immediate and extended family members. Many cultures place great importance in establishing a strong familial relationship with one another. Family relationships are created automatically due to being related by blood. The simple caregiving acts a mother performs for their child, such as carrying or breastfeeding them constitutes part of the relationship building process. If people do not actively build relationships and connect with one another as a family, they may slowly drift apart and lose valuable familial bond.

Romantic relationship

We build a romantic relationship with a person we share intimacy and passion with. These relationships are based on mutual love, care, respect, and affection. A romantic relationship can arise out of friendship or sometimes, from professional relationships.

When we have a better understanding of the different types of relationships, we move towards creating better relationships with people. We can start building relationships with people whom we've never had any connections with before, or find ways to improve existing relationships.

Chapter 19 – Winning with People 1: How to Analyze People

In building a healthy relationship with the people around us, we must be able to understand their behavior and emotions. We can do this by empathizing with or actively listening to them. By actively listening to their words, we can not only show them that we care, but get a better understanding of their personality and motivations. Once we have mastered self-awareness, the process is almost similar to getting to know others. We observe how people react to situations based on their words or actions. A useful method for this is active listening.

In communicating with people, there are verbal and non-verbal aspects of a conversation. These can also be divided further into five aspects: things that are said, things that are unsaid, tone, body language, and words that are used. Active listening involves paying attention to all five aspects of communication. Active listening requires a lot of attention and focus on the listener's part, which requires some degree of practice. Listening actively to a person makes it easier for us to empathize with them. Active listening means showing genuine interest in what the other person is saying. Do not get distracted when communicating with people. When we do not give our full attention to the other person, our minds tend to wander and think about other things, which will usually show in our face or body language.

Active listening also means that we need to put aside our biases and prejudices. Avoid judging, labeling, and criticizing the person you are speaking to. The purpose of active listening is not to judge but to understand them. If you start judging them, you risk making yourself unapproachable and distant.

Asking people questions is an excellent way to show that we are listening to them to gain a deeper understanding. Asking questions also helps diffuse some tension that may be present because it helps them focus on using their logic, which is needed to understand and answer questions instead of focusing on their emotions.

Remember that we listen to understand a person better, not to fix their problems. Of course, if you do have a solution which you think can surely solve the problem, you can offer it to them. However, most of the time, people share their problems just to have someone listen to them. They are not looking for someone to help solve their problems, they just need someone to listen and understand what they are going through. This is a common mistake people make while listening. In such situations, instead of racking your brain trying to find a halfhearted solution, acknowledge what they are feeling and empathize with them by saying something like, "That must be hard for you", or "I really hope it gets better", or even "That really sucks".

Our body language should also be appropriate and match the type of conversation we are having. We should not be having a light-hearted body language when discussing a serious topic. Our body language should indicate openness, flexibility, receptivity, and encouragement.

Try and get the person to talk about their emotions. You can do this by asking more open-ended questions as opposed to yes or no questions. This can also help the conversation flow better and encourage reserved people who do not talk much to express themselves. For example, instead of asking "Are feeling sad about Jennifer leaving the company?" you should ask "How do you feel about Jennifer leaving the company?" We can use reflective statements, statements which convey back to the speaker what they have said.

Chapter 20 – Winning with People 2: Why Social Skills Matter

In the workplace and professional environment in general, having good social skills will always be an advantage. Shy people may have difficulties socializing and tend to keep to themselves in the workplace. They miss the chance to take advantage of getting to know people and getting people to know them. They may have certain skills which could have given them the opportunity to excel in a certain project or department, but because of their lack of social skills, people are not aware of this due to their lack of visibility. The person without proper social skills is then unable to take advantage of their true potential. On the other hand, some extroverted people are anything but shy, however, they lack emotional intelligence and are unable to leave a good impression with the people they interact with. They may be too loud or lack the flexibility to interact with different types of people.

Building a good network of contacts will always help you build positive rapport and can open up more business and career opportunities for you. To build networks, we must be able to socialize and interact well with all kinds of people. This would normally require some degree of self-confidence and emotional intelligence. In the current business environment, there is a growing and greater emphasis placed on teamwork and collaboration abilities. In order to work effectively in a highly collaborative environment, the person should have sufficient amount of social skills to be a successful team member and capable collaborator. Collaboration and teamwork can involve working with people in the same or different departments in a cross-functional team. These teams not only include working with people in the same job level, but also different levels such as managers, leads, seniors, juniors, or intern employees.

It is becoming more common in the past couple of years for companies to engage in inter-company collaborations. It is no longer the case for only one representative of a service provider company to liaise with another representative of a client company. There are now multiple interactions between team members of different companies regardless of their seniority. Inter-company collaboration can also involve business partners, clients, suppliers, vendors, or contractors, where parties from different companies work together as if they all come from the same organization. Therefore, it is becoming more crucial than ever to have practical and flexible social communication skills.

Effective social skills matter because when we work closely with others, we must foster positive interpersonal communications to encourage better outcomes. A 2017 study noted the growing importance of social skills in the labor market. As automation slowly replaces routine jobs, and companies become more service-oriented, there is an increasing need for people with sufficient social skills to fulfill these difficult to automate jobs. While most jobs are being taken over by many kinds of automation, the one thing that computers cannot simulate is the human connection.

Chapter 21 – Winning with People 3: How to Communicate Effectively

Being assertive is another key component of emotional intelligence in terms of establishing healthy communication patterns. It's also one of the most crucial skills required for anyone in a leadership position. Assertiveness is the quality of being self-assured and confident in a positive, calm, and collected manner when dealing with other people. It refers to the ability to stand up for your beliefs without being aggressive. In other words, being assertive is the ability to make a balanced statement which neither indicates weakness nor domination. We can call it flexible control. Assertive people will voice their opinions, direction, or needs in a clear and respectful way. They can easily back their views without being defensive. When instructing or suggesting someone to do something, they do it firmly without being rude. Part of being assertive is also the need to be clear and unambiguous. Here are some examples of assertive statements:

I don't agree with you. This is how I see it...

I will need to think about it. I will get back to you soon. Thank

you for your concern. But I am not interested.

It is necessary to keep in mind that these assertive statements will depend on specific situations. You will need to gauge how to be assertive in different circumstances. It is also important to note where you stand in terms of being assertive in your communication with other people before working on improving this skill. Are you assertive enough or are you too aggressive? There are times when unassertive people try to be assert themselves only to go too far and end up being too bold. This may be the case when you try it out the first few times, but it's not a big deal. As long as you are aware of the results and recognize the need for adjustment, keep practicing.

The difference between assertiveness and aggressiveness is that being aggressive is about fulfilling a personal objective without giving much consideration to the other party, while being assertive is about finding a middle ground. Aggressive people tend to think in terms of winning and losing, whereas assertive people will think in terms of creating a win-win situation. Being assertive also means showing concern and understanding of the other person's feelings and preferences. Even if you do not agree with their opinions, you still need to respect them. An aggressive person may say, "You are clearly wrong," but an assertive person would say, "I have a different view about it. If you can't agree with me, we'll have to agree to disagree." When refusing or disagreeing with someone, just remember to always be respectful. Doing this shouldn't be difficult if you can be calm and put your emotions aside. Aggressive people also tend to focus more on winning or gaining rather than resolving a particular problem effectively.

Assertiveness isn't just about not being shy in expressing your needs, opinions, or goals whenever it matters, but being able to stand up for your principles and values. When encountered with situations that they have strong opinions about, assertive people will always make themselves heard without being too harsh, dramatic, or condemning. For example, you overheard a conversation between two colleagues about "loose women" from a particular state, which you found repulsive. You need to tell them it's not a nice thing to say, especially at work. There is no need to be overly hostile. However, keeping quiet about it can mean that you don't mind people having such conversations in the workplace.

How to be more assertive

An excellent way to learn to be more assertive is to practice in front of the mirror. Preferably, use a mirror which is big and clear enough where you can see your facial expression and body language. Imagine having a conversation with colleagues or friends and think of a topic to talk about. You can talk about planning where to go for lunch, deciding on an activity to organize for the team in the next social gathering, or discussing how to go about completing a certain project. For example, your colleague wants to remove a section from a report both of you are doing together. You believe that this section should be included. How can communicate this in a polite but assertive manner? Think about the choice of words to use, your tone of voice and body language. At the same time, imagine yourself in your colleague's position. Think about how he would feel. Will he feel offended or insulted? Is he coming any nearer to seeing your point of view? Practice a few times, making appropriate adjustments.

When working with someone, whether a subordinate or someone on the same level, you must view them as someone who you need to work with and not against. Avoid competing with people; aim to cooperate and collaborate with them. This is essential when working with people in the same team, department, or company as you. This can also be applied to when working with people outside your organization, such as clients or suppliers. Show them a healthy amount of respect. When you think about working with them instead of against them, it is easier to be assertive.

Remember to remain calm at all times. We have discussed how to control and manage your emotions in earlier chapters, and now we need to use this ability to be assertive without being aggressive. Being assertive requires you to make objective evaluations about the situation and the other person's state of mind and opinions. It would be difficult to make these evaluations if you are feeling emotional. If you're unable to remain calm, there is a high chance of being too aggressive and offending the other person. Try and keep your composure by maintaining the proper posture and eye contact, and speak in a steady manner.

Get into the habit of using "I-statements." This will help you to state your opinion about something without making it sound like an attack against the other person. I-statements can help you sound more assertive and at the same time, respectful of the other person's space. You can use I statements whenever you need to inform the other person about how you feel about an issue. It is intended to show the other person (assertively) what you need and not what they must do. I-statements can be used when we disagree with someone, need to confront someone about their behavior, are unsatisfied with something, or when someone else is not happy with us. Starting the sentence with an I statement instead of "You" can help lessen the accusatory tone of the statement. For instance, instead of saying, "You should have consulted me about it first…" you could say, "I feel that I should have been consulted first about…" or "I did not appreciate not being consulted first about…." By using I statements correctly in the proper context, it can help you be assertive without unnecessarily raising the other person's defense mechanism.

Do not feel guilty about refusing something or standing up for your beliefs. There is no harm in being assertive about how you feel when something does not match with your values, priorities, or needs. When you are engulfed in guilty feelings, like refusing to attend a party because you weren't in the mood, instead of thinking what a useless friend you are, think about why skipping the party was the right decision. Maybe you wouldn't have had a good time there anyway, or you didn't want to spoil the mood for others at the party, or even that since you can always make it up to your friend another time, she will surely understand.

Chapter 22 – What is Manipulation, How it Works

So far we have learned about how to understand the behaviors and emotions of other people and communicate more effectively to build positive relationships with them. Also, we've learned how to read people's feelings and respond to them in order to be in good standing with them so that they'll have a positive opinion about us. Lastly, we learned how to establish communications with people that are more natural and effective. Moving on to the next level of EQ, we will learn about manipulation. Manipulation may seem like such a strong and negative term because it is often associated with bad behaviors. But not all manipulation is wrong, such as positive manipulation.

Many of us may have practiced positive manipulation or engaged in it a few times in the past. Manipulation refers to the practice of influencing a person with the aim of inducing them to do something or think in a certain way. Manipulation can be seen in practice almost every day by politicians around the world. A dishonest politician may manipulate the public into believing that supplying weapons to corrupted dictators is encourage-able. The difference between positive and negative manipulation is the motive behind it. It's clear that selling weapons to irresponsible people is wrong and therefore, would be considered as negative manipulation. What about the case of selling weapons to honest and responsible foreign leaders? Some people may think that manufacturing weapons in itself is wrong, let alone selling them. Others may believe that selling weapons to sane and responsible people is okay.

Manipulation can be done through different techniques such as lying, omission, denial, rationalization, seduction, playing the victim, guilt-tripping, diversion, evasion, and many more. Manipulation can further be defined as the act of persuading another person with the intention to fool or control them into doing something that results in them being harmed.

Persuasion, on the other hand, involves less dishonesty, more transparency, and is intended to put the person being persuaded in a much better position.

Here's a scenario concerning e-cigarettes or vaping. A politician is trying to convince the public about the dangers of vaping, assuming that vaping indeed has health complications but very minor ones. Pro-tobacco lobbyists approached this politician and asked him to promote the dangers of vaping with the goal of stopping the decline of cigarette sales in the country. The politician then instructs his team to find anything they can on the dangers of vaping no matter how minor or unlikely. This would be considered negative manipulation because the politician's personal gratification motivates the main goal. Now, what if all the facts remain the same except that the dangers of vaping are very real, and the risks are very high. Arguably, it's still negative manipulation because the politician intends to capture monetary gratification. But if we look at the bigger picture, the public would also benefit from this advice because now people are aware of the dangers of vaping and can take steps to avoid it if they wish. Therefore, it is all a matter of perspective. If the issue can result in something positive, perhaps there is no real need to oppose such manipulative actions. If, however, both the aim/intention and the results are negative, then the manipulative act is negative and should be avoided altogether.

There are many benefits in learning both negative and positive manipulation. By understanding the mechanics of manipulation, you will be able to protect yourself, as well as the people around you from getting manipulated, and you'll be in a better position to detect and expose harmful, manipulative behavior in the workplace. Learning the art of persuasion can give you better control and influence over the people around you, which will mold you into a better leader, one with the ability to direct subordinates towards better results. It will also give you the ability to motivate people more effectively, especially through challenging situations

It is worth recognizing that emotional intelligence can be potentially abused or applied in the wrong way. Manipulation is one of the most common ways EQ has been used to further undesirable agenda. The goal of improving our emotional intelligence is to improve ourselves not only to become better leaders or team members but also to become compassionate and empathic people. Therefore, we should be aware of the pitfalls involved in learning EQ and steer clear of it.

Chapter 23 – Mastering Positive Manipulation

People may have a brilliant idea about something and may naturally feel that others should be able to see how indeed brilliant this idea is. Unfortunately, it would take a lot more convincing than merely showing a heightened passion in an idea. Most of the time, people are occupied with other issues or are just skeptical about things in general. Sometimes they only see how something can benefit them in the short term without considering the long-term gains. Working in sales will require a lot of persuasion skills. You will need to convince potential buyers why they should part with their money to buy a product they're unsure of. There might even be times when you need to persuade or manipulate yourself into thinking in a certain way because of long-held beliefs or deeply entrenched prejudices to gain long term benefits.

In all these scenarios, you could use your persuasion skills to get other people to see things from your perspective. Certain matters may only require minimal persuasion while others may require a higher degree of it. It's important to understand the essential basics of the art of persuasion and to do a lot of practice.

Personalizing the message

Whenever you need to persuade someone into adopting your point of view, always personalize the message to fit them. You need to understand your audience before you can begin convincing them. Whether you are speaking to the warehouse workers or the company board, tailor your message to suit their needs. You may be dealing with your colleagues, people from other organizations, or with public customers. Sometimes you may be dealing with a group of creative people as opposed to logical or scientific individuals.

Target the correct people

Persuasion may take up a lot of energy. Therefore, choose who you want to pitch your message to wisely. On the one hand, there are people who you know are very easy to convince or are in fact already convinced. You may not need to do a lot of persuasion with this type of crowd. On the other hand, there is a group who you know is almost impossible to convince due to their background or circumstances. There may be no reason to expend energy to persuade these folks. The key group to look out for is the people who do not see your point of view yet but has at least some potential to be persuaded.

Focus on the benefits

Most of the time, people are only thinking about themselves. You need to frame your message in a way which highlights what is in it for your audience. For example, if you are selling a banking product over the phone, you need to get the message across clearly on how the customer can benefit from signing up to this program. If you are selling internet service, you must convince them what benefit they would get from terminating their current internet subscription. Clearly, in both cases, people are only interested in how much money they can save or gain. When you are pitching an idea, you need to highlight the benefits to individual team members or the company.

Take note of the timing

People tend to change their opinions throughout time. An idea which might have sounded preposterous ten years ago may not seem so bad today, just like there are certain periods good for investing.

Believe in what you are proposing

Be confident and certain about what you're suggesting. You're going to have a tough time convincing others when you yourself are not sure about the idea or product you are selling. Others can easily detect uncertainty in your facial expression, voice tonality, or body language. You must be 100% convinced yourself about the idea you are pitching before you can effectively persuade others.

Stay calm at all times

Conflicts may arise during heated discussions, especially when people are passionate about certain topics. Emotions are bound to flare up during discussions. Some people may easily get offended merely by the words you use. Therefore, remaining calm in situations like these can be advantageous. You learned how to control your emotions in difficult situations earlier, so use this ability whenever you need to persuade a difficult audience in buying into a controversial idea. Staying calm not only helps you think clearer and respond better logically, but it also helps you appear more confident and convincing to your audience.

Be prepared

The more complex and detailed your proposal is, the more time you need to prepare yourself for the pitch. You will need to cover all grounds surrounding your idea. For example, if you need to persuade a panel why they should hire you for a position, be prepared to know about the position, the company, and their products as much as possible. When you are proposing an idea for a project, be ready to address all the possible concerns people may have about it, including the non- obvious ones.

Be clear

Some people are so passionate about their ideas that they allow their passion to cloud their judgment and have difficulty explaining it in a clear and orderly fashion. If the concept involves something very complicated or convoluted, take the time to simplify it down to some basic fundamental points. It is also good to pace yourself depending on the complexity of the idea as well as on the mood of the audience. You need to gauge the sentiment of your listeners. If you are going too slow, they might get bored and their minds may wander. If you are going too fast, they might miss some crucial facts and may misunderstand your presentation, or they might get lost entirely about what you are getting at. Try not to be cryptic if you can avoid it.

Be persistent

Persistence demonstrates conviction and sincerity. It also helps to reinforce the value of your idea, especially if it's very novel or unconventional. Sometimes it takes a lot of patience to convince people about something. Abraham Lincoln had a great vision for the country since early on in his political career and had to endure multiple rejections and failures. But Lincoln kept on persisting and as a result, managed to be elected president of the United States where he was able to carry out a vision that forever transformed the country. Most of the time, we need to repeat our points frequently in both written and verbal form to ensure that the audience can truly digest the message.

Create a sense of scarcity or urgency

When you have selected the perfect time to suggest an idea, it is important to instill some kind of sense of urgency or scarcity in the minds of the listener. If they are not motivated to buy into your idea now, it is less likely that they will have the motivation to buy into it in the future. This sense of urgency usually relates to timing. The time to take action is now because if you wait any longer, the circumstances will no longer be the same and new factors may come into play. This sense of urgency does not need to be absolute. You do not need to fix some kind of definitive deadline. There may be a small minority of listeners who are inherently more cautious and need more time to digest your idea fully. As long as you make them aware of the need to act quickly, there is a greater chance to win over your audience.

Close the deal

Once you've managed to get some form of agreement from the listeners, affirm it back to them through your words and actions. It's even better if you can get them to confirm their agreement verbally in front of the other listeners. When you can persuade just one person to agree to your idea, the chances of influencing the others will improve tremendously.

How to Influence People with Mind Control and Neuro-Linguistic Programming

Neuro-Linguistic Programming or NLP was invented by Richard Bandler and John Grinder in the 1970s as an approach for communication, psychotherapy, and mind control. In other words, it's a method for performing light hypnosis using verbal communication for manipulation or persuasion. NLP uses both verbal and non-verbal linguistic patterns to trigger desired responses in the subconscious mind of the respondent. Since then, NLP has been used widely in hypnotherapy, marketing and advertising, and political campaigns, just to name a few. NLP techniques require in-depth training and understanding. Here are some of the most common and useful methods used by NLP practitioners.

Paying attention to the person

NLP users pay close attention to the person who they wish to influence. They will look at their body language, eye movements, pupil dilations, nervous tics, or breathing pattern. These features can normally give clues as to the person's state of mind and be triggered in response to questions, or any statements or words used by the practitioner.

Emphasizing keywords

NLP practitioners often use certain keywords to elicit a particular reaction from the other person. These words are usually suggestive and sometimes permissive. Suggestive words typically relate to the human senses such as "sight", "hearing," or "touch" in order to suggest something you want them to follow. NLP practitioners also use vague words to distract or overload the conscious mind to tap into the person's subconscious thinking.

Building rapport

Building rapport with another person can help improve their communication and responsiveness towards your suggestions. Building rapport can be done by mirroring the body language, voice tonality, or body language of the other person. Once you have established this form of rapport, it's easier to lead the other person into your way of thinking or convince them into accepting your ideas.

Recognizing Negative Manipulation

Having a healthy level of emotional intelligence can help us detect manipulation. Although we're familiar with all the many different emotional states that may arise from different actions such as guilt, shame, pity, or anticipation, we still need to understand how manipulative behavior works and what the signs of manipulation are. Negative manipulation can be revealed using many different techniques.

Asking for an immediate answer

Manipulators will often expect you to give an answer quickly as a way to maximize control and pressure over you. They tend to do this when you have somehow bought into their idea partially but not entirely. They will use all sorts of guises to create a false sense of urgency, such as claiming that the offer they're presenting you may no longer be available after today.

Giving the silent treatment

When you give someone the silent treatment by unreasonably not answering their calls or text messages, it creates doubts and uncertainty in their mind and throws them off balance. Manipulators need to constantly be in control and maintain their psychological superiority over you in order to carry their schemes effectively. So you can use this technique to break their patterns.

Guilt tripping

Manipulators will sometimes make you feel guilty about something as a way to ease you into buying their ideas. Manipulators may press on about how much you will lose by not agreeing to their way of thinking, or raise the fact about how much effort they have gone through to meet you and explain everything to you.

Assuming your intentions

Manipulative people often voice what they assume you're thinking about and use it as a means of control over you. More often than not, these assumptions may be correct, which can throw you off balance. The ability to understand people's thoughts and emotions is indeed a sign of emotional intelligence, but using it in such a way is very intrusive and manipulative. These assumptions can also be false, but the way the manipulator says it might cause you to think that it's true.

Flattery

There is no denying that being flattered feels good, but some manipulators will use flattery to exercise influence over you. An expert manipulator will know how to flatter their victims by not blindly complimenting their physical attributes. Any flattery which seems out of place should be easy to detect, but if one is not careful enough, they might still fall victim to it. It becomes harder to detect manipulative flattery if they complement something about you that you find believable. For example, a feature that you feel slightly insecure about, but have put a lot of effort into improving. Therefore, it is always better to be cautious whenever you receive a compliment. Be meek but polite about it. A simple thank you should be a good enough response.

Hinting at your weaknesses or insecurities

Manipulators may often remind you of your insecurities or weaknesses by indirectly referring to them in the form of humor or sarcasm to make you feel inadequate and inferior so that they can maintain their superiority. They may even sometimes criticize or judge you directly when the situation calls for it. They will also try to make you feel like there is something wrong with you to push you off balance.

Aggressive behavior

In some situations, manipulators will behave aggressively towards you if they feel that there's a chance to intimidate you as a means to gain superiority. They may do this by raising their voice, making big gestures, or displaying strong negative emotions verbally.

How to Avoid Getting Manipulated

By recognizing the typical techniques used by manipulators to manipulate people, you should be able to guard and free yourself from getting manipulated. Here are some other tips which you can use to handle the situation better in the future.

You have rights

When dealing with a manipulative person, it's important to be aware of your rights, and realize when they're not being met. So long as you're not hurting others, always stand up for yourself. The following is a list of your basic human rights.

- You deserve to be treated with respect.
- It's your right to voice your opinions, emotions, and needs
- Don't be afraid to say "no" when necessary
- Always assert yourself whenever you feel like you're being mistreated
- It's okay to have opinions that are different from other people
- Never allow others to take advantage of you physically or mentally

These basic human rights describe your boundaries. However, most manipulative people will deny you these rights so that they can control and exploit you. Be that as it may, recognize that you're the one in control of your life, not the manipulator

Stay away

One approach to determining if you're dealing with a manipulator is to observe whether they put on different faces in certain situations. Although many of us are guilty of this to some degree, manipulators are particularly skilled at this to an extreme level, such as being friendly to one person while being utterly disrespectful to another — or being absolutely vulnerable one minute and aggressively hostile the following. When you notice this kind of behavior from a person frequently, stay away from them unless you absolutely must confront them. The cause for this kind of manipulation is complicated and deeply rooted within the person, so do not attempt to change them. It's not really any of your business.

Avoid playing the blame game

Since the manipulator's vendetta is to take advantage of your failures, it's reasonable to feel deficient and take the blame for their behavior. However, the issue isn't with you; you're basically being influenced to feel awful so that in your moment of weakness, they can take advantage of you. Think about your previous encounters with a manipulator and ask the following questions:

- "Am I receiving fair treatment?"
- "Is this individual's request rational?"
- "Does this relationship feel one-sided?"
- "Do I like being a part of this relationship?"

Your response to these questions should be insightful enough in helping you confirm that they're the one with the issue.

Refocus the attention on them

Unavoidably, manipulative people will make unusual demands that require much effort on your part. When you receive these irrational requests, return the attention to them by asking some simple questions like:

- "Does this sound fair to you?"
- "How am I benefiting from this?"
- "Do you seriously expect for me to do this?"

These questions reveal their true character and intentions. If they're smart, they'll likely retract or back down from their request. However, more aggressive manipulators, like narcissists, will ignore you and assert themselves in their demand all the more. In this case, here are some tips to regain your rights and throw the manipulator off balance.

Make the best use of time

Not only do manipulative people make unfair demands, but they usually require you to answer them immediately. Rather than giving them a timely response, break their influence over you by giving them an ultimatum, such as, "I'll think about it."

Think about how dominant these few words are from a client to a sales rep, or from an attractive woman to a thirsty beta male, or from you to the manipulator. Take the time to assess the advantages and disadvantages of the circumstance, and whether you'd like to take a more aggressive course of action by saying "no," which drives us to our next point:

Assert yourself by saying "No"

To almost certainly say "no" strategically but firmly is solid evidence of your communication skills. When done correctly, it enables you to stay grounded while keeping the relationship professional. Remember your rights (saying no when necessary and preventing others from taking advantage of you).

Suffer the consequences

What if the manipulator refuses to take no for an answer and is keen on abusing your rights? Then let them suffer the consequences. Being able to set consequences assertively is a crucial skill needed to bring down a troublesome individual. When verbalized successfully, it can stop manipulative people dead in their tracks, and force them to shift their personality from abusive to respectful.

Confronting abusive behavior

The manipulator may use intimidation any time by threatening you with physically. But be mindful that they only abuse those they regard as being weaker, so if you continue accepting rude behavior from them, you become their target. But most abusers are cowards, so the moment you assert and stand up for yourself, they usually back down. This same rule that applies to bully/victim situations in school also works in office environments and workplace settings.

Part 6: Emotional Intelligence in Practice

Chapter 24 – Practical Exercises

Have periodic breaks from social media

If you spend a lot of time on social media sites, make it a habit to take periodic breaks to go offline once in a while. This will give you more opportunity to interact with people outside your home, school, or work and improve your emotional intelligence skills. While practicing these skills online can help you in certain areas, to truly expand your EQ abilities, you need to interact with others face to face. Many aspects need to be worked on such as your body language and voice tonality. Furthermore, in real life, you can't actually delay your response for too long unlike when communicating online.

Listen to your intuition

Sometimes, we may be faced with a tough choice and are unsure of how to make a decision. Our intuition can play a decisive role if we need to break the stalemate. It may also be the case where we've already decided what to, but our intuition says otherwise. While you listen to your intuition, always analyze them consciously before acting on it just to be sure that it's the right judgment.

Read more fiction

Studies have found that reading fiction can help readers develop more empathy because when we read about other peoples' lives, we can easily put ourselves in their position and imagine what it'd be like being in their shoes. As we read more books about people from all different walks of life, we can understand them in real life better; not merely those who are close to us or in our circles, but also a more extensive variety of people.

Hang around people who don't normally agree with you

People usually stick with individuals similar to them in values, age group, race, gender, political views, or social class. As the saying goes, birds of the same feather flock together. While this is important in helping you establish your bearing in society, you should aim to associate with people from different backgrounds who may not always share your views. This can help you widen your horizon and learn about other people's perspectives. Staying exclusively in your own echo chamber will not encourage improvement in your emotional intelligence because everything will always be predictable. Mixing with different groups will help you understand more about yourself and can give you the opportunity to better control and manage your emotions in unfamiliar settings.

Chapter 25 – How to Use Emotional Intelligence Skills in Real World Situations

There are many areas where we can apply emotional intelligence in our daily lives, such as at home, work, school, or anywhere else. Remember that most of us have been using our EQ with almost everything we've done throughout our lives. It's just that the level of EQ that we've been using is not nearly our full potential. Having a high EQ means that you're able to recognize and acknowledge your weaknesses and limitations in term of everything that you do, including the limits of your own IQ and EQ. Therefore, the goal should be to improve your EQ by maximizing your full potential instead using it to get ahead of others. We should work towards competing only with ourselves, and no matter where we stand on the scale, there is always room for improvement.

We have covered many examples of how emotional intelligence skills can be used in the workplace, such as building positive relationships with colleagues, superiors, or subordinates; as well as establishing connections with the people outside of your organization. Ultimately, it increases your chances of having a successful and fulfilling career. You can start implementing the many skills you've learned in various aspects of your life.

For instance, if you have children, one of the skills you can use in raising them right is to motivate them to work harder in school. If your children are very unruly and often get on your nerves, your emotional intelligence can help you control your anger and channel it in a healthier way. Raising children is no easy task and takes a lot of effort, and most parents without emotional intelligence will find it difficult to overcome these issues or be completely clueless as to how to solve them. Having emotional intelligence can help you overcome these difficulties by helping you manage your emotions as well as your children's to find a rational solution to the problem.

In terms of relationships, emotional intelligence can help you understand your partner better and connect with them on a deeper level. Emotional intelligence can also help you peacefully resolve conflicts without blowing up issues into something bigger.

In school, emotional intelligence can help you build rapport with your classmates and teachers. It can also help you make the learning experience in school more worthwhile for yourself and those around you. Moreover, you can become a great leader or team player by having a substantial amount of emotional intelligence.

Conclusion

Emotional intelligence can open up a whole new world of opportunities and excitement in your life. It doesn't matter what level of emotional intelligence you have right now; you should always strive to improve. Emotional intelligence can not only empower you with essential skills for success in life, but it also guides you in becoming the best version of yourself. As the world continues to evolve, re-affirm your commitment to making positive changes in your life. Begin working on your action plan if you have not done so already. Remember to always be patient as there may be times when you feel like giving up. When those times come, remember that only through hard work and perseverance can you make positive changes. We wish you all the best in life and in your journey to becoming a more emotionally intelligent person.

Once again, thank you for reading Emotional Intelligence Mastery. If you enjoyed this book or received value from it in any way, then I'd like to ask you for a favor: Would you be kind enough to leave a review for this book on Amazon? It'd be greatly appreciated!

To leave a review, just go to: **ReviewEQ.com**

If you enjoyed Emotional Intelligence Mastery, then you'll love the previous book in this series called **Cognitive Behavioral Therapy**.

Go to: **CBTbook.com**

GET YOUR COPY TODAY!

also available at
amazon.com

Printed in Poland
by Amazon Fulfillment
Poland Sp. z o.o., Wrocław